The Morning Regaining Her Glory

The Morning Regaining Her Glory

The Morning Regaining Her Glory

A sexual trauma survivor's journey to poetic justice

Belle Jar

White Carnation Press

www.themorningregainingherglory.com

Illustrations and cover design by Belle Jar

ISBN- 978-0-578-21726-0

Dedicated to all the women who never 'asked for it.'

I document my pain.
I am my own science experiment.
For maybe if I share
This burden I silently bear
Someone else out there
Will recognize herself in me
And she will know
She is not alone.

When she doubts
Her place in this world
Following what happened to her
I want my words
To validate her
To reaffirm—
This world is still her home.

If you read this
And it speaks to you
Whether it be
A shout
Or a quiet whisper
Know I believe you
And I am proud to call you my sister.

The Morning Regaining Her Glory

Table of Contents:

Trauma
Is not organized.
Healing
Cannot be defined—
As something linear.

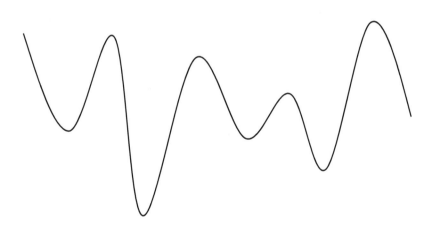

The Morning Regaining Her Glory

Preface

8/6/18

My soul is so full. How can it be that this bounty of blessings bathes me after a decade it feels of drought. Once I took the leap off the ledge I feel as though, my soul has been dipped in destiny's gold. And better yet I feel this is only the beginning. That I am meant to do great things, see great things, to be great. If my younger self could have seen me now she would perhaps understand that it had to be — all her suffering, to lead her to where I now stand. And I hope with a full and fastidious heart. I want to leave a lovely mark on this world. My critics may call it a scar, graffiti. Whatever they please. But my soul is a mural that longs to be painted. Dripping ink from the toes on my feet. Drawing lines only to cross them. Building up my walls to turn them into art. Welcome to my museum.

Acknowledgements

My sister, for picking up the phone and telling me what to do at a time I could not access my mind. For making sure I did not give up or go home. For dropping everything to cross the sea and rescue me.

E, for waking up and being by my side—being my voice and my guide during that long night. For all the love in the days after.

M, for the countless hours in hospital buildings and the police station. For endless hugs and my favorite explicit translations.

A, for the immense compassion and beauty you have within. For making me believe truly good people still do exist.

L, for being my first friend overseas and believing in my crazy dreams. For encouraging me to sing in front of strangers, watch jazz musicians, and talk about major philosophy players.

H, for embarking on this journey with me across the sea. For never being afraid to talk about feelings. For keeping me company on my lonely last days and making sure that I never give up writing.

Z, for showing me how strangers can become your sisters in a matter of weeks. For being my travel buddy. For embracing my every whim—even the ones that sounded crazy.

My brother, for taking me away to momentarily escape in the San Francisco Bay. For calling a counselor for me before I had even returned from overseas. For being a big brother who has always supported his little sister's art and writing.

Mom and Dad, for showing me I am worth the cost of trying for justice, even if the odds do not always seem favorable. For allowing me the freedom to try to create something good from something bad.

X and V, for giving me a place to stay when I did not feel safe behind the walls of my bedroom. For every Sunday lunch, at which I felt a part of a family.

My therapist (A), for being a true friend and being willing to stand by my side in court room proceedings.

My counselor (J), for helping me understand and learn how to physically heal from trauma. For refusing to let me blame myself.

L, M, D, and T, for reminding me of who I am at a time I had forgotten.

My lawyers, for not settling for anything less than justice. For fighting for me while I heal overseas.

Introduction

I used to think
I was waiting for
My time to bloom.
That I was the Morning
Before her glory.
I thought I must open up
In order to bloom
But that was
A dangerous truth.
It was not until
They robbed me in the dark
That I could finally see:
The glory had been there
All along
Rooted—
Inside of me.

I am the Morning regaining her glory.
This is not my tragedy.
This is my story.

Most girls learn
They are not the exception
In a typical fashion.
The charming *caballero*
Turns out to have
A line of ladies in his queue.
They may think they
Are worth *more than that*
But he is skilled at
His balancing act.

I learned in a bit of a different way.
My ears first learned
I was not the exception.
My body was next.
I should have trusted my ears.
They were sirens
I could not comprehend.
The blood came too late.

I wanted to believe
In fairytales.
How could I be
So naïve
To not see
Monsters too—
Come with golden scales?

I used to lie
On my bed at night
And look up
At imagined stars.
Now I cannot sleep
Unless I am on my side.
It seems like *I*
Am the only one
Who is on my side.

How do you believe yourself
When women tell you
The bloodstains you bear
Are lies?

A million eyes in sight
To air out your dirty laundry.
Left to leave
The crime scene.
Forced to flee
The country
Where you have carved
Your dreams.

Not wanting
To be a victim.
To let them take your drive.
But the car is stalled—
You cannot move.
A traffic jam
Inside your mind
While they are free to cruise.

What are the odds
I can ever get even?

<u>Things I can no longer do:</u>

1. Wake up to a pink, light-filled room.
2. Watch parades from my balcony.
3. Visit the man in the black beret at the jazz store.
4. Fall asleep to the sounds of my roommates on the couches outside my bedroom door.
5. Join my roommates on the couches for evenings filled with endless laughter.
6. Walk to the nearest supermarket and purchase a sleeve of chocolate-filled cookies and nothing else.
7. Have staring contests with strangers on the metro.
8. Order chai lattes in Spanish from my favorite coffee shop, only for the barista to immediately switch to English.
9. Chat up the Scottish bartender at my favorite café.
10. Imagine my artwork on the walls where they were set to hang.
11. Think up ways to invite the Scottish bartender to my art show.
12. Chicken out and order a cappuccino each time.
13. Plan my showers down to the last minute before the hot water fails, and I am left under icy streams.
14. Run down to the school cook to ask what I can eat for lunch that day due to allergies.
15. Usually pout when I see my options.
16. Sing in front of strangers on Wednesday nights.
17. Form a band with a select few of those strangers.
18. *Trust anyone ever again.*

Am I a fool to think
I was ever owed
Anything
From this universe?
To think that
The more pain I bared
The greater the gift would be
When she finally
Made her presence known
And dropped the world
At my feet?
I thought I had seen
The worst of things.
I thought the most
That could be stolen from me
Was my wallet.
I thought the only things
That could mark my skin
Were the bed bugs bore by
My mattress.
I thought the only thing
That could take advantage of me
Was an institution
Not a *he.*

How wrong could I be?
How wrong could I be?

I stand in line
At the pharmacy.
Waiting
For the pills
To help me sleep.
To calm this inner anxiety
That has not left
Since he touched me.

The pharmacist smiles
And hands me
Un regalo para Navidad.
I look down to see
Female intimate gel
Staring back at me.
A voice inside my head
Laughs silently
Because although the universe
Is undoubtedly a bitch
She has a sense of humor.

Misunderstanding

She writes to me
It was just
A misunderstanding.
Did I misunderstand
Lying limp in the dark?
Was I confused
In the intention
Of the invasion
She did not witness?
Yes, I was confused.
Confused as to why
He killed the lights?
Why I could not see
Where he was
Until he was inside?
And even then—
Could only imagine
The foot of the bed
Where he stood
Head held high.

Did I misunderstand
How he kept on
My shirt
My pants
And my shoes?
Only pulling them
Down far enough
To do as he so choose.

How can it be?
The one girl to see
Through my brave facade
Later switches
Her integrity off.
Do not go to the police.
It was just
A misunderstanding.

Tell that to my sister
I called in tears on the street.
Or to the marine
Who did not answer the phone
At the American Embassy.
Tell that to my roommate
Who I shook awake
Traumatized by
The look on my face.
Who went with me
Without question
To three hospitals
And endless police stations.
Tell that to the men
I was made
To try to explain
Over and over again
In a foreign tongue
All of the things
I could remember
He had done.

Tell that to the pills
I must take to sleep
And to all of the needles
They stuck inside of me.
To the swabs invading
My most personal place.
To the intrusive memories
And those that have been
Permanently erased.
Tell that to the girl
Who kept to herself.
To the girl who was
Going to leave
Before he had the chance
To do this to me.
Who decided to stay
Because she wanted to believe
The good in people.
She wanted to believe
The good in you.
Tell me now.
Tell me please.
That this was all just
A misunderstanding.

When the lights went out
Inside that room
I swear the lights went out
Inside me too.

Graduation

I thought each day
Would get a little easier
But each sunrise
Seems to grow darker.
I must say goodbye
To the women
Who have become my sisters.
To the women
Who held me together
When the seams of my body
Began to give.
To the women
Who gave me their strength
With no strings attached.

How I hate to cut these cords.

I must part
With city streets
Which house
My most treasured memories
From the distant
And recent past
Though they now seem
Long-coated
In funeral ash.

I walk on the cathedral stairs
In front of the King's palace.
A street violinist plays
The graduation song.
I mimic the walk of students
Filling in the arena.

Perhaps—
I have graduated
From this terrain.

But I have nothing
To show for it.

Good Surprises:

Puppies
Cupcakes
Gift cards
Free shipping
Phone calls from old friends
Winning lottery tickets

Bad Surprises:

Sex

Rough Draft

Sometimes my mind wanders
Far enough away
That I think perhaps
It is possible
To flee my body.
To take flight
With the pigeons at my feet.
But I come back.
My mind migrates
To the present
And I wonder
How I could have spent
So long—
Sitting up on the wires
Planning my future
For it to become my past
In an instant.
A camera flash—
Except I do not want
Any of these polaroids.
These reminders
Of what could have been.
Of the life
I had wanted for so long.

It feels as though
I had it all drafted.
Thousands of words
Chapters
Promising storylines
A happy ending
Only for the computer to crash
Before ever pressing save.
What will you do next?
They ask
But my page is _____.

25

I thought the first time
A man entered my body
He would knock on the door.
I thought the first time
A man entered my body
It would be the first time
He saw me
In my original state.
Not needing rose petals
Nor candles
But at least
He would keep the lights on
To see my face.

But it wasn't like that
You see?
He did not choose me
For anything besides
Vulnerability.
He just sought
An empty space
To occupy—
To dominate.

At the time I only had one
But now my body
Is an empty vessel
Which nothing can fill—
But shame.

I almost did not
Meet up with you.
I was relieved
When you did not
Look like your pictures.
I figured we would meet
For an afternoon drink
And call it quits
But it was you
Who would insist
On wanting to see
More of me.

I gave you outs
Ways to leave
But you passed these
Tests with flying colors.
I wonder now
Was it all an act
To get me comfortable enough
To keep his crimes
Under covers?

Maybe one day
You will use me
As an anecdote on a date.
To joke about the dangers
Of meeting strangers online.
As though I was the dangerous one.
Dangerous in the way
I almost got away with
Delivering justice.
Peligrosa
For making him rethink
Possibly slipping something
Into my drink
Till' I was hazy enough
That he thinks
I will not remember.

And the girl sitting
Across from you
Will laugh
Wanting to believe us girls
Are 'all crazy'

-For the sake of the dimples in your smile.

My eyes are
an ocean

———

but I am
a shell of
who I once was.

Wolves in Designer Sheep's Clothing

I met a boy
Who—
To tell you the truth
I was not very interested in.
But he seemed to be
Very interested in me
And like many other girls
I liked this feeling.

When he came back around
I was giddy.
When he came back in town
He invited me
To a gathering
He previously
Told me all about.

But it was not anything
Like he had claimed.
Not like the videos
He had showed me
In the café.
But like many others
I tend to people please.
Like many others
I am guilty
Of wanting people
To like me.

Please—

Cast the first stone
If you too
Have never wanted a group
To like you.
To fit in
Someplace new.

A few drinks in
A few uncomfortable
Truth or dares later
He pulls me into the kitchen
To let me know
He is interested in
Another girl there.
A girl who is in town
For one night.
A girl who is engaged.
Confused, I—
Ask if *I should leave?*
I gather all my things.
I am ready to walk away
But they stop me
Telling me to stay—
To be confident.
A challenge, I accepted.

I wish I would have known
These people were not
Looking out for me.
That they would later go on

To exploit my vulnerability.

30

The Chamuyero
Walked around the table to me
Planting a kiss on my lips
Without warning.
He was dared
To kiss who
Ever he wanted to
But this did not sound like
A dare to me
But rather a way to kiss a woman
Without asking.

You taste like wine
He said.
I wonder why?
I faked a laugh
Pointing to
My glass.
Trying to hide
I was cringing
Deep inside.
Believing that this
Would be
The only unwelcome advance
That evening
But it was just the first.

In a matter of hours
I went from emotionally vulnerable
To physically vulnerable
And I cannot help
But see
How the two connect.
I curse myself
For the times I would watch
Brené Brown
And her Ted Talks.

I did not see the abuse
That can attract itself
To you—
And your heart's willingness to be open.

Yes I know
It should not
Be marked my mistake
For placing ripe trust
Among rotten men
Who project a false face.

There is no one
With the foresight.
No psychic
To predict
The horror of that night.

I have learned not all demons dance in hell
And the worst of them know how to decorate well.

I wanted to learn a language.
I wanted to learn a culture.
I did not want to learn them both
Through police reports.

-Be careful what you wish for.

Stripped from
My self-made homeland
I cannot fathom
The thought
Of stepping foot
Back in the closest thing
I have to a bedroom.
Looking at the photos
Of a girl I once knew
Staring at me on the dresser.
Apologizing
For failing us both.
For having everything
She worked hard for
Reduced to nothing.
Feeling as though
I am walking back in time
Except this time
All which kept me moving
In the past
Was the thought
Of a future
I now know
I can never have.
And that smiling girl
In the photos
Is lucky she does not yet know
It could not last.

I do not know
Who I would rather be.
She?
In the photos
Blissfully ignorant of
The fate which awaits her.
Or *me?*
Unable to look at
Couples holding hands
Under Christmas lights
Along the street.

Payasasa   *Clown/Fool*
Asquerosa   *Disgusting*
Hija de puta   *Son of a bitch*
Drogadicta   *Drug addict*
!Llama la policía!   *Call the police!*
Te voy a cortar el cuello   *I'm going to cut your neck*

-Things Romeo never shouted at Juliet's balcony,
but my rapist shouted at mine.

Victim's Interrogation

They kept telling me
I was brave
For everything I had done.
As though it took courage
To seek justice.
To want the man
Who robbed you
Of the life you earned
To pay interest.

It was not until
I was sitting
There—
In that police chair
For the second time
In seven days
Counting down
The fourth hour
Of questions.
Of probes.
Men telling me
You're losing.
We have no DNA.
He was careful.
This was a rehearsed play.
You have no witness.
The only man I knew
Was possibly in on this.
This was his home.
These were his friends.

We need more.
They pushed me
To go back
But I had nothing
Left inside.
It was as though
They wanted me
To lie
Just to give them something.
Yet each time
I told the truth
They warned me
Cuidado—
A judge will read this too.

Why couldn't you
Have held your hand
Out the window
To capture
The yelling man
On the street?
Why do you suppose
They had something to do
With this threatening?
I too live
In the noisy, city streets.
What compelled
You to press record?
Why couldn't you
Have produced
Better audio?

They asked
Seemingly annoyed
As I covered my ears
To avoid *that* voice.

Three men standing
As I sat in a stiff seat
Telling me
Details I remembered
Weren't compelling.
They would not count
As evidence
In a case
Like this.
And I realized
The men who I thought
Ought
To fight for me
Deep down
They too
Wanted to believe
This was all just
A misunderstanding.
Wanting me to deliver
The evidence they need.
To put in the time
To make *his* crime
Convincing.

Were you on your period miss?
You know virgins
Tend to bleed?
We have a million cases
Just like yours
He pointed to a shelf
Of files they would never read.

We need more.
All everyone did was take
When I had nothing left.
Demanding I remember
When all I wanted to do
Was forget.

You closed down the shop.
More or less
They said
At the end.
They put on their backpacks
And headed home—

Just another day at the office,
friend.

Metamorphosis

On my back
Like a cockroach.
It was the closest
A woman has ever been
To Gregor Samsa.
And I think
He is the only man
Who could remotely understand
What it is like to be a woman
Helpless—
In this position
Under an unbelievable circumstance
To which nobody longs to listen.

I used to think
You men formed
Strong pillars of the community
But I realized
Hands used to pluck roses
Can only belong
To men who are *weak*.
You may have washed off
The blood of my thorns by now
But I will make sure
The scars never leave.
You will spill
Rose petals from your mouth
A constant reminder of me.
The sharp thorns
I speak
Will pierce your peaceful dreams.
If I must live in a nightmare
During the hours of light
I will rob you of your right
To a smooth slumber
Each night.

If I can no longer
Lie on my back
I will make sure
You live on yours.

-You will learn you stole from the wrong garden.

You thought I
Would right
Your wrongs
But you
Must have misheard.
I will write
All your wrongs
Stitching back
My wings with words.

They told me
They brought you in
For questioning today.
I wonder if you realize
The reality of the situation
In the bed where you now lay.
But I think all is
Lost upon
You as you continue
To go on
Swiping.
Finding other ~~women~~ victims.
Will you invite them
Just to break them down too?
To tell them
You have found
Something new
On their three-minute walk
To the party door?

The most wicked
Part of my brain
Dares to wonder
That maybe if I had been
Enough for you
If I had worn my hair
In a different way
Or made up my eyes
With a different shade

Maybe—
You would have
Seen me
Worthy
Of protecting.

You invited me into
A monster's den
And I understand now
If I wasn't worthy
Of your protection then
How could I ever expect
The words you say now
To make things
Right somehow?

And you probably used
Your dating apps
In the police waiting room.
After all—
They brought you in
To town for the weekend

And you are not one
To miss out on a good time.

The lawyers called
To tell me
My case has been
'Provisionally dismissed.'
My hands
Scramble to the search bar
Faster than my heart
Manages to race.
They say
We have two days
Left to appeal.
The courts claim
The reason is
I did not identify
His face.
But I remember
Climbing the stairs.
I remember
The stiff office chairs
As I signed my name
Like a receipt across him
As if—
I was ordering justice.

-I still hope it will be served.

Today I found
Your friend request
Along
With all the calls
And messages
You had sent
When I thought
I had removed myself
From the one web
You could not tangle me in.

There may have been a time
When my stomach
Would float
With butterflies
At the sight
Of your name
On my screen.
I did not realize then
You had only floated moths
Inside of me.

It was different
This time.
I read messages
Never to reply.
Only to learn
More lies.
Guilt fired
At me.

You try to plant
Bad seeds
But you should know by now
This garden
No longer welcomes weeds.

You said you
Did not understand
Why I was doing
This to him.
Was it all
To hurt you?
And I wonder
Which is worse?
Whether it is
A script slipped
By lawyers
Or if—
You are that large
Of a narcissist
You think I would
Subject myself to all of this
Just for the sake of spiting you.

One makes me laugh
But they both make
My insides weep.
Learning people like you
Exist
Outside of bedtime stories.

I think at first the sea of strangers
Awaiting the arrivals of their loved ones
Thought I too was crying
At the joy of coming home.
Something in their faces changed
When I persisted to pass by
Unable to mask tears and blotchy eyes
Under the guise of something good.
My brother saw me
And I knew he did not know
How to make sense of it.
I walked in front of a family photo
Unknowingly
And dropped my luggage at my mother's feet
As I continued walking.
She was waiting for me outside of the bathroom stall
Arms embracing me
For what felt like an eternity.
It was as though I had not been able to feel
Anything at all since that day.
Occupied with doctors and lawyers.
And more doctors and lawyers.
But once that plane touched the ground
And I was back in the place
I never wanted to return
Stripped of my dreams
And everything in between
I felt everything all at once.

I cannot watch most TV
Or listen to any music.
I used to live for it.
For the lyrics—
Its poetry.
But now it is too much.
Heavy reminders of love
And its seeming simplicity for others.
Reminders of the purest joy in life
That the universe would decide
I not only did not deserve
But should be punished
Beyond repair.
And I wonder who I was
In a past life
Or who I wronged
On this life's journey
That tilted the scales
In a way that I was deserving
Of being broken three times
In one night
And chipped
On each night which followed.

I do not know
If I will ever feel normal.
They took more from me
Than security.
Than the ability to trust.

It is the mental warfare.
This battle
They will not cease to wage
For me to shut up.

To accuse me of the crime
Of reclaiming my power.
To paint themselves
As victims
With paint from my palette.

I always aim
To see the good in people
But these people only aim
With the intention of firing.
I am the roadkill
They did not expect
To stand up and start walking.

Family money
You use
To carry out
And cover up
Your crimes.
But with all of this
Spare change
I only think it is only right
For you to pay.

-You are in your victims' debt.

I Understand

I understand now
Why women stay silent.
I thought it would be
Different for me.
I called
My embassy.
I did not walk
I ran
To the police.
Doctors poked
And prodded me
But still I am a statistic.
Reduced to
Just another number.
Just another file.
Another pair of
Bloody underwear
Sitting on a shelf somewhere.
If I can do
Everything I did
And still get asked
Why I did not resist?
And still have my case
Provisionally dismissed?

If I can get told
It is '*a shame*'
I had to lose my virginity
'*This way*'
But I better get up
And on with my day
Like nothing ever happened.
While he gets up
And gets dressed for work
I desperately search
My dresser drawers
For self-worth.
For the strength
To distract myself
From the hurt
Long enough to try
To begin to plan out
The rest of my life
As the country and court
To which I continually cry
Abandon me
And defer my dreams

Making me feel as worthless
As my attacker.

You try to manipulate me.
You think you can tap into
The heart I used
To wear on my sleeve
But I have since hid it away
Ever since the night
I learned of the danger
Which lies
With vulnerability.

Predators sniff out empathy
Like a bergamot candle.
Ready to burn you
Under the guise
Of making light
But they should not take
This lightly.
Fires that smell sweet
That may reside
Beside claw tub baths
Still have the power
To burn down houses
And everything in their paths.

Bad people do not always look
The way you would think.
Sometimes they wear designer suits
And have properties lining the beach.
They may take pictures next to luxury cars
Holding up expensive cigars
But there are not enough dollar bills
That give them the right
To touch you against your will.
There are not enough cents
That allow them to look past consent.

-Please never forget this.

My students asked
About me today
And I wonder what they think.
What the school would say
To explain—
Why I vanished without a trace.

Right now
I could really use
Their suffocating hugs.
Right now
I could really use
Their abundance
Of unconditional love.
Right now
I could really use
Their thick-accented
*You are very beautiful*s
Parading down the halls
At a time when
I do not feel

Worthy of love at all.

Epiphany

I do not know why
You have always been able
To read my mind.
Across the sea
And the web online.
You noticed
Things had changed.
Just in time
You called my name.

I do not know how
To express enough thanks
For the words you wrote
Which spoke to me
Though be it typed
In a scream
At a time
When I felt
So defined
By the echoes of strangers.

The words of these villains
My shame allowed to creep
Until you made it clear
Nothing I could ever say
Would change—
The way you saw me.
That you know
Me thick-and-through.

That is when I realized
I had been trying to win
The validation
Of poisonous
Women and men
Who will never truly
Know me
When I have ripe people
Like you—
Who do.

I spent too long
Looking for validation
From the men
Who attacked me
And those
Who did not intervene.
I thought if I could get them
To understand their wrongs
Maybe my heart
Would start again
And I could move on.

But I was foolish in my pursuit
In asking my monsters
To tuck me in at night.
In asking arsonists to stop themselves
At just creating candlelight.

I learned spineless creatures
Will not bend their backs
To yield to the truth
And psychopaths are incapable
Of feeling anything—
Except the walls inside of you.

What I wore
Did not matter.
I have been
More scantily-clad in church.
He did not care
For nudity.
Removing my clothes
Would have meant more work.

This was no
Two-for-tango.
This was
A one-man show.
He did not
Have time to waste.
He did not care for
Stage lights on my face.
What more does it require?
To understand rape
Is not about lust
But *power.*

He could have had her
If he had decided.
I could detect their chemistry
From the moment
I entered the scene.
Perhaps—
That is why
I was so unsuspecting.
Perhaps—
That is why
She was so quick
To turn on me.
Perhaps—
It invoked
Some sick fit of jealousy.

But she refused to see
I was not chosen
In a beautiful
Mutual
Way.
I was not his lover.
I was vulnerable.
I
      was
         prey.

You do not know
How to
Let loose
My roommate said to me.
I believe—
Her literal translation
Had been
You do not enjoy life.
That I was uptight.
The two of us
Are very different
She would say.
Don't worry.
It is okay.
Though her eyes
Said a very different thing.
When she demanded
My roommate explain
My empty room
After I ran away
She questioned whether
I had been exaggerating.
She said she did not know
How *she* would sleep
Knowing what
Had happened to me.
Yet she had no problem
Taking the things I had left behind.
Though she may be wearing my sweaters now
She did not send me
So much as a goodbye.

The hardest part of this
Is knowing he will never feel sorry
For what he did.
That he would only regret
Not getting away with it.
Only upset—
That it weakened
The confidence he had
In his dark intelligence.
In his ability to carry out a crime
Without baring the weight of it.

I want to heal
But I am constantly reminded.
Made sick to my stomach
By the medicine I must take
To protect the house
He broke into.

Though he has been evicted
The nausea remains
A box on my doorstep.
And each time
I open this door
I am met with the fear
He has left
An unwanted delivery.
And each time
I must remind
Myself I am safe.
Saved by other pills
They made me take.

My body has converted
From a temple into a pharmacy.

There is no religion.
Still I am cross.

Though broken
I continue to break down.
Unable to accept
I was chosen.
Unable to accept
I could not fight back then.

Enraged enough now
To heat my body's
Former frozen state
But it is too late.
It is too late.

Losing Hand

I cannot look
At decks of cards anymore.
They remind me
Of sitting around that table.
The more I reflect on
What remains
In my memory
The more
I see
This round table of men
Were not knights
And I myself
Was a card to be played.
Intended
To end
Up in someone's hands.
Passed around
Like a secretive bet.

I had always thought
Of myself
As a queen
But looking back
I see—
I was the joker all along.

Payasa
They screamed
Down my street.
It is true.
I am the clown
For I did not see
The cruel fate
They had planned for me.

And my heart aches
Having to accept
The hand it was dealt.

I wonder how people like you
Manage to sleep.
How you hug your little sister
On Christmas Eve.
The one with a similar name
The one with the same age
As me.

And I realize
There is a reason
She is never invited
To parties like these.
And I wonder if she bears
A similar secret to me.
One she could never tell you then
And would not dare tell you
If she knew
What you do to women who speak.

Ode to the Narcissist
I Kissed (Pt. 1)

You are like
A little boy
Needing the flashes
Of their smiles
In your direction
To feed
Your need
For constant validation.
To feel
You have
At last
A path.

You do not
Even need
Us to undress
To feel
You have achieved.
I could tell
By the way
You poorly kissed me
And copied cheap lines
Stolen from movies.

You just need
To put on
A good enough show
For women to clap
In your direction.
A noise
Perhaps your ears
Have fallen deaf to
Your whole life.

But deep down
You and I
Both know
You don't
Feel worthy of the applause.
That you are nothing
To be celebrated alone.
You mirror
Our brightest parts
Desperately wanting
To claim them as your own.

Ode to the Narcissist
I Kissed (Pt. 2)

Perhaps you do not see
He uses you.
Playing you
Like the instrument
You are too lazy to adopt.
To reel us in
And groom us for him—
The perfect victims.

For when you
Are done with us
Is when he acts.
But he does not
Put on a show
Or fake the role
Of the hero.
He studies you
But he is not your understudy.
He does not
Pretend to be your substitute.

He uses your own narcissism
To bait us
When our wings
Have been wounded
By your words.

Perhaps I am his last victim
But you will always be his first.

I was just target practice.
You wanted to witness
How many shots
You could make.
You wanted to test
How many bites
You could bait.

I should have known
It was not cupid's bow
Pointing at me.
Once I made it out alive
I realized—
It was catch-and-release.

He wants girls
To marvel at him
Like he is the moon.
He holds his head sky high
Because he is terrified
Of being found out by you.
It is obvious
But he tries to hide it
From all of us—
That his light
Does not exist.
He is nothing but
A projection.
He wants to be
On a pedestal
Because to knock him down
Is to see
He never had any light.
The sun gave him
Everything.

I had finally
Been settling in
To my chosen home.
He decided
To settle into my body
Why couldn't he have just left me alone?

My brother finds me a fool
To ever believe
I can return
To the country I was
Forced to flee.
He does not think
This family
Will let me waltz back in
And live my life freely.

But what he does not know
Is that at
This point in my life
I do not suppose
I would put up
Much of a fight.

They have already killed
What was inside.
Still they have the nerve
To ask me *Why?*
As though he is
The victim
And my tongue is the crime.

My hair falls out
In brown ribbons now
Like streamers
At the worst goodbye party.
And I wonder how
He still manages
To take more away from me.

I learned something
I never wanted to:
Your body recognizes trauma
With or without you.

-Still, they will claim things like this was just 'bad sex.'

I am trying to cope
I promise.
I hiked nine miles
To prove my strength
Looking back
At the San Francisco Bay.
I walked along the surfers
At Mission Beach.
Still,
There is not enough sand
To fill this hole inside of me.

I try to distract my mind
To keep it from wondering
Until I see a sign
On the street
With your name
Or the city from which
Your bloodline reigns.

And I wonder
When a trigger
Does not take me
Back to that room
Or the constant shame
And self-ridicule.

I wonder who is
The bigger coward?
The people who saw
The fear on my face.
Who heard—
The accusations I made
And let me leave?
Or the girl who spent
The entire Christmas day

Fast asleep?

Bystanders

You beg a woman
In the bathroom
Not to approach the man
Who forced himself on you.
You want her help
Not vengeance.
Afraid of him
You do not want
To attract attention.
But she does not listen.
She goes instead
To pay him a visit.
To yell at you after
Calling you a liar
In the kitchen.

A few people ask
If you are okay.
You say you are fine
Though your hands
Visibly shake.
Though there is fear
Written across your face
To them
It is a foreign language.
Though you are
A disheveled mess
With eyes that cannot hide
Preoccupation
With his occupation.

Though they have heard
The speculation—the claims
Nobody stops to investigate.

Later you cannot decide
Whether your body
Or your mind
Was in greater shock.

70

I will never understand why
He was able to change her mind.
Maybe they too
Tangled bodies that night
While I laid in a hospital bed
Legs spread wide.
And when my lawyers call
To ask her why
She can tell them all about
My attention seeking that night.

She has pictures at the women's march
But when I went to her for help
She marched to my rapist.

It was like I was a child
Begging the devil
On his playground
To explain—
Why he touched me.
Not wanting to be
The problem child
Creating chaos for *anybody*
After he wrecked *mine.*

Her reaction had been
So disorienting
I went to him
Hoping—
He could offer words
To prove to me
That this was not
What we both knew
It was.
That monsters do not
That they cannot
Surround me.

In that moment
My voice pleading
For a reason
An explanation
But he told me
Nothing besides
It's best if I leave.
His face vacant of emotion
His eyes revealing
He was truly empty.
Not in a way
Which tells you he is aware
He is lacking something inside.
That something key
Is not there.
But the kind
That sends a crippling chill
Down your spine
Through the air.

My body is a solid
But my god
I do not matter.
Lately I have been
More liquid
But thank god
I am 50% water.
That it would take
Too long to empty
What remains
Left of me.
But is this a curse or a blessing?

-I wish I could evaporate.

I wonder if there
Will be a time
When my mind
Is able to think of
Something else.
I wonder if there
Will be a time
When I am not
A hamster on a wheel
Running back and forth
Both chasing
And escaping—
Anger and sadness.
I wonder if there
Is a way
To stop these tears
Without drowning my body.

I wonder if there
Will be a day
I can fully accept
And be okay
Knowing
I was not worth saving
To any of these people.
I wonder if there
Will be a day
I can accept
That I was worthy.
That I am worthy.
That it was they who failed
Their most basic human duty.
That it is they
Who are not worthy
Of my forgiveness.

-I wonder.

I do not know if you feel shame.
I know you wanted me
To be—
Your dirty little secret.
And yes—
There was a mess
But I am not the one
Who needs to wash their hands clean.

Judas

I want her to know
She is guilty.
I want her to know
If she had done the right thing.
If she had helped me
Escape safely
My chance at justice
And this PTSD
Would likely be
A very different story.

That we could have told
A different tale.
One of sisterhood
Of putting the nail—
In his coffin.
But she would rather be
His disciple.
I want her to know
She will have to
Scrub her hands clean
Of every victim after me.

-I hope for her sake, she is not next.

Where do I go
From here?
Everyone tells me
I have somewhere to go
But this life feels without purpose
And no one—
And no place—
Feels like home.
I am living for the sake
Of keeping others comfortable
Knowing my heart still beats
Within an arm's reach.

It would have been easier
If he would have
Put a pillow
Over my head
The moment I tried to speak
Because then I would not be forced
To answer my father
When he knocks at the door
Following another seventeen hours of sleep.

How do you balance
Not wanting to give them
The satisfaction of killing you
With not wanting to breathe?
How do you balance
Relentless insomnia
With not wanting to do anything
But sleep?
How do you scream at them
That they are
In the wrong
Without making a peep?
How do you demand
They listen to your voice
The way they forced you
To listen to the screams
They sent down your street?

They say the devil is in the details
But he works hard to make sure
You do not remember most of them.

Chewing Gum

I had a pit in my stomach
The night I saw
He blocked my number.
An act of calm
Before the approaching storm
I called my sister
Paranoid
Of impending thunder.

It was as though
My body knew
I could not sleep
Through—
The night.

Two hours into
A hazy snooze
I woke
Scared to approach
My balcony
Even in
The absence of daylight.

That voice
I will never wipe
From my head
Still greets me
In the middle of the night
When I toss
And turn in bed.

My bones
Will never forget
Trembling in unison.
They are coming for me
I sensed
And fled my home
Fearing violence.
Wishing
I had cherished
The moments in which
I previously owned
Rent-free—
The feeling of safety.

In that moment
I knew
You were all
Truly sick
To send a threat
Like this.
Before you knew
I had paid the police
A visit
You sent—
Reinforcements.

In that moment
I knew
You did not expect me
To wake up
With you still in the room.

I
      bet
You did not expect
Your sharpest tools
To fail you
But they did.
I remember your face
Signing—
My name
Upon it
Like I was issuing
Your death warrant.

I
      bet
You did not expect
Such bravery
From a meager girl
Like me.

Though I may have been
Paralyzed by fear
Back then
I am not afraid
Of you anymore.
They can leave the partition
Outside the court room.
I want *you*
To look me in the eyes
As you spit lies
Like gum you have chewed on
For far too long.

But just as you
Grow tired of gum
That loses its flavor
Society grows tired
Of predators like you.
I will end up
On the board of directors
While you end up
Gum
          on
                my
                      shoe.

This country
Which claims to be
Far removed
From its fascist history
Still allows your rapist
The right to lie
On the stand.
To turn your trial
Into a creative writing contest.
Rewarding him—
With freedom.
If he can craft
A convincing short-story
He is let off the hook
Without so much as a slap.

Another day
Another trigger.
I cannot believe
You have an angel's name.
It is ironic.
It is sickening.
I am puking out words
Left-and-right
Like a child trying their hardest
To talk their way out of trouble.

Another day
Another sign.
Your country
Your language.
It follows me
And I am running
But I cannot keep up pace.
I run to the edge of Sunset Cliffs
And for a moment
I think of jumping
Until I hear sirens
Coming to rescue
Someone who has fallen
By mistake.
And I find it
So unfair.

Why is it so easy to die while alive?
But so hard to kill yourself
When inside you are already dead?

I still have big dreams
But now I am aware
The world is not
What it once seemed.
Sure, tomorrow is
Not much different than yesterday.
The difference is
I have changed.

-I now see (all that hides) in the dark.

I apply to jobs
And imagine a life
Where I can pretend to start over.
To carve a new path.
One with footprints
That nestle my bare feet
Like a baby cradled
In her mother's arms.
And though 'x' marks the spot
On the map which failed me.
The one I hung upon my wall
For a whole year
Wishing
To make this city my home
I must realize
I am my own treasure map.
I just have to reach
Within myself
To find the gold
Fools failed to steal.

I wake up in California.
I feel the heat from the sun
On my back
In the middle of December
Yet I am cold to the touch.
I wake up to bright lights
And kisses from dogs
With poor manners
But I feel like the stray.
Wandering the streets.
Looking for a promising home.
Unable to find a welcome mat
With the right saying
Enticing me to stay.
I walk the streets
Wailing inside.
Looking for a pack
With a vacancy my size.

The people who let you down
Are not always
Monsters on the street
With track marks
Dotting their arms
Like metro stops.
Sometimes the people who
Drop you—
Not caring if you break
Your neck along the fall
Are the people who
Could have been
Your role model.
People who
You could have
Aspired to
Be like
In another life.
And it sickens you
Because though you know
These people are nothing
To look up to
At all—
There are young girls
With their images
Lining their bedroom walls.

-*The (in)actions of women hurt just as much as those of men.*

Thank you for being
An angel in human form.
For clearing your schedule
To help create a sense
Of calm within me
After this violent storm.
More than a shrink
A true friend.
Not trying
To type my trauma
But to simply listen.
To point out the choices
I still have in this life
At a time
It seems I am stubborn
For wanting to
Be free to go left
When they say *it's for the best*
I go right.
I am sad that I no longer can
Sit across the room
When I talk to you
And accept a glass of water
From the kitchen tap
After you drop your child off
At another woman's flat
But I am so happy
I can still speak to you
Through a screen
Across the ocean blue.

Across the time zones
Your digital shoulder
To lean on
Has meant the world to me.
At a time when
Everyone looks at me
Like I am a fragile doll
Reminding me
That I have been
Greatly broken—
You remind me I am strong.

That I am more than
Just cracked porcelain.

-An open letter to A .

Everyone cares at the moment
But soon they will return
To their lives.
My father will take flight
Returning to routine
Alongside
Spreadsheets and salmon.
My brother will achieve
The start of his
Graduate school dreams.
My sister will continue
Her search for a new apartment
And smile at texts
From the new man in her life
While my brother
Spends his nights
At his new girlfriend's place
To try to keep his happiness
Out of my face.
And I will eat vegan ice cream
On the upholstered couch
Alone
Browsing postings
For entry-level jobs
That require five years of experience.

-Reality check.

Nothing on the TV
Scares me anymore.
True life provides more fright
Than horror films.
I no longer fear ghosts
But instead
The intrusive thought
That it is more often
Than not
The people you think you know
Who are possessed by
A shadow side.
Who express a hidden evil
In the absence of daylight.

I gave out trust
Like a leaking garden hose
But I watered weeds
Posing—
As trees.
Their shade
Was not the kind
You could stop and rest under.
Their canopy
Was a coverup.

I learned this world is a masquerade ball.
One in which you never know
If one is using their mask
To hide poison or protect gold.

I am trying to rebuild my life
But it is not as simple
As a Tetris game.
Things do not simply
Fall into place.

I can no longer
Live my life
By the mirage of manifestation.
Of positive thinking.
That only
Left me
Vulnerable—
        Bloody—
               And naïve.

A queen expecting
No one to attack
An unguarded palace.

I must lift up the drawbridge.
My moat has been
Flooded with
Too many tears.
I must ban white knights
For the rest of my years.

The California waves whisper
Sweet nothings to me
At a time when
Villains' voices roar.
They drown out the lies
Of the men who
Will not let me part my lips
But forced apart my thighs.

I am not usually prey
But he has always been
A ~~sexual~~ predator.

Gerrymandering

I see people on the internet
Everyday
Who receive death threats
For poorly-construed tweets.
For their bad beliefs.
140 character—
Lacks-of-integrity.
But I don't want you
To lose your job
Or your right
To a happy life.
You see
The evil that runs rampant
In your bloodstream
Was not engraved upon
This heart inside of me.
But *I want you to wake up*
Each day knowing
The disgust I hold
For women like you.
I want you to wake up
Each day
And replay—
In your mind
Your starring role in the scene
That invades mine.
That intrudes my thoughts
And sleep-less nights.

How can you justify
What you do?
They preach
Believe all women
Why couldn't you have
Believed *me too?*
A woman in her thirties
While I was a naïve
Twenty-two.
With a well-seasoned career
That I would have aspired to
If I had not
Known the truth
About the disgusting devil
Living inside of you.
A woman who
I made
The mistake
Of running to
For help.
For protection.
Who decided to
Turn the tables around
That kitchen island
And shout
How dare you?
A woman who punished me
For seeking her help
After a crime.
A woman who made
My rape
About her

Who switched in seconds
To believing my predator's lies.
Who shamed me publicly
Traumatizing
My memory-loss-laced mind.
Leaving me
Hanging.
Wringing me out dry.
Airing out
My bloody
Dirty laundry
In front of a room full of eyes.
Who did not even
Blink twice.

Tell me
Did that score you a visa?
A residency?
A job?
Or simply
Some points with
The business school boys?
So self-serving
Your collision in my life
To you was likely
White-noise.
But I'm here to teach you
A powerful lesson:
You will never tune out
Another woman again.

-An open letter to the woman who shamed me.

Esperanza

They claim they will
Reopen my case.
They say
It was a mistake.
But I do not understand
Why it took
The same police man
To whom I had spoken
Two-weeks
To avoid handing in
The documents denouncing
My attacker.
And I realize corruption
Is not a rare road
In this machismo-driven land.
That it was not
Too long ago
That it was ruled
By a crooked man
Who got off
On the same power trip.

Women's rights
He stripped.
Poetry's greatest minds
He whipped
Into permanent
Silence.
And I hope if Lorca
Can hear me
He sends help my way
And a poetic verse
Of the need to nurse
Justice—
Into the ears of men
With the power
To bring about just change.

He is written into
My manuscript
Though he is less
Than half of it.
You do not have
To sift—
To dig
To uncover him.
He hides
In plain sight
Mirroring his actions
From that night.

I do not write my story for attention.
I do not want to be forever known
As the girl who was a victim.
I do not want
To be reduced
To a sound-bite
In the news.
I just want
To make the write moves
So another girl
Will never have to
Look back on the same fate
That I do.
I do not care
If reliving my worst fear
Through writing
Leaves me tortured
For a longer time
If it means
I can intervene
And try to put an end to an era
Of gender-based crime.

This weighs on me enough
Yet still I cannot resist
To entertain the thought
Men will now view this
As too much baggage.
How do you ever trust?
Once you learn
Dangerous people seem
Capable of love.
How do you ever explain?
The reason which lies
Behind—
Your fear of intimacy
Without sending men
Running.
Men think they need
To be afraid
In this day and age
Of a woman
'Crying rape'
But this is not
The case.
How can I
Communicate?
Though I am good
I am not damaged goods.

This is my cry for justice.
This is my scream
At Times New Roman's
Loudest decibels.
Can you hear it ring?
Like the freedom I deserved
To enjoy a night
Without having my body touched
By more than words.

This is my written wail.
I am contorting my face
Like a Picasso.
Can you hear these keys
Scream—
Louder than Munch?

I sit here a woman
My mind active in logic's war
Wondering
Why it is so hard
To avoid unwanted attention

But so easy to have your wounds ignored?

Punctualidad Americana

My life changed
At the touch of a button.
One might suggest—
The butterfly effect.
Though I had butterflies
Floating in my stomach
The moment I saw
An invitation to accept
From a boy I thought I knew
More or less
I had no idea
To expect
The nightmare which
Awaited me.
That I would sink
On the city's boat street.

Climbing up
That set of stairs
For the second time
I had that same feeling
Of butterflies
But soon it would
Drop off.
By the time
I realized
They were only moths
I had passed
The point of no return.

Perhaps there was something
Different in his eyes
This time.
Something that
I failed to see.
Perhaps when he
Opened the door
I was a punctual delivery.

Appraisal

You have the most beautiful
Set of eyes
Mine—
Have ever seen
The Chamuyero
Said to me
But you wear
Too much makeup
He critiqued
As though my face was
A work of art
But inherently wrong
For being
A painting.

But I did not choose
To be part of a gallery
That night.

The more time
Went by
I began
To realize
I was a part of an auction
Set up by the one person I
Thought might have become
My future collector.
But he told me
He had his eyes
On a new shiny prize
And sold me off
To the highest bidder.

I was just
Too young to see
The museum into which
They had recruited me.

I will not let them
Devalue my stock
As a woman.
My value only appreciates
As I invest in myself
And in others.
And even when
I make mistakes
The lessons I learn
Boost my interest rates.
Your family deals in
Precious stones
And yes—
I am unique
But I am no
Commodity.

-Your influence in my life will soon be buried as low as your
underlying insecurities.

It is not your fault
This world has fault lines.
They may shake you
But you still stand
The test of time.

You are not to blame
Your body is a pacifist.
It does not mean
You ever asked for this.

Your open heart
It—
May have made you a target.

He may have left you
In ruins
But know this—
You are not ruined.

-A message to the woman who feels guilty for her
  body's biological response.

If the chest
Which houses
Your heart
Starts to feel
Less like a home
I will drape
Strings of light
Around it
To spark your soul.
But please do not
Evict yourself
From your body.
I will help you
Pay the rent.

-To all the women who need to hear this.

I am a woman
You want as your ally.
It is dangerous
To underestimate
What I would do
To expose the truth.

I am a woman
You do not want
To misjudge
As delicate.
I am equipped with
Silent resilience.

I am a woman
Whose tongue
Is sharper than the swords
Formed—
From Damascus.
Trust me when I say
You do not want to be
On the other side of the blade.

User Agreement

I am going
To be okay
Though I have cried
Three times today.
I realize
I can fantasize
About someplace—
Someone—
Or something
Coming along and fixing me
But none of that exists
Yet happiness
Is in reach—
In my midst
If only I would turn my eyes
Within.

No amount of ocean beach
Or pensive thoughts
Of New York City streets
Or imagined London callings
Can return the feeling
I was lacking
Before and after
He violated me.

I must agree
To my own
Terms and conditions.
I must respect
My own privacy
Giving myself permission—
To grieve
The loss of the girl
Who used to live
Inside of me.

I have learned
There is no point
In 'sharing'
Unless it is aimed
At showing others
That you too
Leak.

There is no point
Placing band aids on the soul
If the blood on your heart
Has not yet dried.

I must go
To the doctors again.
They must poke
More needles in my skin.
Did you know
It has been
A month
And still—
He has not been called in?
Did you know the files
The courts need
For confirmation
Magically never make it
To their destination?

-Why do I speak to ~~deaf~~ corrupt ears?

I am beginning to learn
There is no such thing
As justice.
For women
We often observe
This is the way it
Just is.

Every day
Is judgement day.
I thought the friend
I have had
Since I was thirteen
Would never question
How much—
I had been drinking.
Or how much—
I had eaten.
She says she believes.
That she knows it is not
'Like me'
But then why do I feel
I am back in front of the police
Subjected to
More questioning
Over coffee I cannot drink.

-This sickness in my stomach I can no longer blame
on the pills I am taking.

Society
Cannot accept
The concept
Of rape.
We refuse to believe
More monsters live
On top of the bed
Than under it.
We blame the women
Because deep down
We want to believe
That sexual assault
Is just a misunderstanding
But the truth is
A harder pill to swallow
Than Plan B.
Trust that
You can take it
From me.

-It seems like the only proof I have in writing.

I cannot tell you
The eye color
Of the man who stole my virginity.
I cannot recognize his voice
On an audio recording.
But I can tell you that he
Graduated with an masters degree
The same year I was still
Ineligible to go to the prom.
When my mother still refused
To let me drive on the highway.
When I was stressed over
The *practice* SAT.
I can tell you he works
In strategy.
It is almost as though he
Had this all planned out.

-Who would have thought?

I used to be so ashamed
Embarrassed by virginity.
I thought it was
Something to 'get over with'
But *not* like this.
This was never my intent.

And I scoff now
Cause it does not count.
For centuries
Society has scored
A woman's worth
By nonsense.
I cannot prove it.
I cannot use it
As evidence
That I did not
Nor ever would
Want this.

-Immaculate misconception.

Disclaimer

Attention seeking
Men scream from keyboards.
How can you be upset?
They would say.
The best thing
To ever happen to you
Was your rape.
But I do not seek fame
From this page.
I seek healing.

I write not out of want
But out of need.

-I'm sickened I even have to put this here.

Misunderstanding (Pt. 2)

You say you do not understand.
We both have that in common
My pending Facebook friend.
Do you know
How horrid it is
To not remember more
Than disconnected memories?
Each puzzle piece
Of the perverted war
He waged inside of me.

You must understand
The pain which resides
In escaping a room
Confused—
Not knowing how long you were inside.
To not know
What someone did to you
Aside
From the seven second intervals
Your mind decides to preserve
As you leave your body
And seemingly Earth
But it is not a high
At all.

My friends called me their muñeca
But that night I was his rag doll.

I am not the type of girl
Who likes to do things
Alone.
I bring my friends
To the grocery store
To avoid buying ice cream
On my own.
If I ever thought it possible
To end up behind
That closed door
As a crowd continues to socialize
Right outside
You better believe
I would not have arrived—
Alone.
If I ever thought it possible
To lie lifeless in trauma
While the man who invited me
Twirls girls in circles
In the living room down the hall
I would never have accepted
His invitation at all.
I did not think
To watch who poured my drinks
At an initial gathering
Of less than eight
Until it was far too late.

-It is more than friend requests that I cannot accept.

I spend my days longing
For a time machine.
The doctor says
It is PTSD
But I am not a soldier.
But just like the men
In the Middle East
I am not the same girl I was
Before I went overseas.
I cannot view
This world the same.
My lens has shattered
And it all seems in vain.

Do you know how hard it is?
To see the men who used
And abused you
Share a new song from Spotify
Or update their cover photo
While you cannot write them
To ask them why
They did what they did to you.
When you cannot respond
To their staged pleas
To 'understand'
When they know why
You went to the police.
When you cannot demand
He tells you
He does not know
He is a vile man.

Do you know what it is like?
To discover
The name of woman
Who traumatized
You so greatly
You forgot
Only to learn
The weekend
That ruined your life
Was one of
Her favorite times.
That she spends her holidays
At peace by the sea.

That she just happens to be
The sister of
A celebrity.

Do you know how hard it is?
To want answers.
To want to know why
Or when they looked at me
And decided *Yes, her.*
To know why no one
Helped me during or after
Demonstrating this was
Something I deserved.
It is almost as hard
As trying to believe
My trauma counselor
When she says to me
These are predators
And everyone else there
Was a coward.

-Why do I feel like the only
prey?

Each day seems
Like a nightmare
Until the sun retires
And then come
The night terrors
And I cannot decide
Which is worse?
These bottles of
Antidepressants
Seem more useful
As noise makers.
Pinches in my heart
All the time
Painfully remind me
I am alive.
I am angry during the day
Especially when
I wake
Having to wage yet another
24-hour war of existence.
But at night
I cannot rest
And the sadness
Surfaces
In waves.

I sit by my bath tub
And I imagine
If I wait
Long enough
I could fill it up
With all the tears.
Longing for a way
To change time
Or at least lose my mind
Long enough to forget

This is my life.

I want the happy poems.
The *it gets better's*.
But this salt in my tears
Has not turned sweet yet.
I have not been met
With the understanding of
A sun on the horizon line.
What is moving on
When *on* is undefined?
How do you draft a life
When your building blocks
Have been stolen?
These are the challenges
I must face
For I refuse to let them win.

I do not know why
It has taken me this long
To realize
None of the poems
I have written to you
Even matter—
Even wound.
For no narcissist
Nor psychopath
Can ever grasp—
A feeling.
Shame can permeate
My every
Cell membrane
But a narcissist only knows
Feeling in vain
Not his veins.
His nerves can only
Transmit self-praise.
And a psychopath
Can never enjoy
A true laugh.
He is as hollow as
The test tubes
I must fill each three months with blood.

Perhaps I have been writing
To no one this whole time
Or perhaps
I have been healing myself
Line by line.

As a poet
You think I would have been able
To read between a narcissist's lies.
To get out in time.
I admit there were red flags
But as I said before
I am a poet.

I mistook a sidekick
For a hero
And the value of a villain
As zero.
I knew they were counting cards
But I did not know
They were keeping score.
That my body was about
To become a scripted war.

They can call me an actress
But it is not my fault
Nature coded my body
To be a pacifist.
It does not mean
I ever asked for it.

Perhaps the crowd thought
I was seeking drama
But this was not an act
It was a (crime) scene.

-And I was cast without ever auditioning.

My counselor says
I likely entered
A state of trauma
The moment I crossed
The threshold
Eight hours before
He stole—
The deed to my body.

She says
The discomfort in the air
Would have been too much
For my brain to bear.
Retreating to its reptilian state
As I caved to their dares.
This testing of boundaries
To which I was unaware.
I could not discern
What was a cultural difference
And what was a cause for concern.

I had my own students
But it was I that night
Who would learn:
Many jokers come dressed as kings
But the wild card has many more
Tricks up his sleeve
And you cannot tell who he will be—

That is his greatest strategy.

A Letter I Wrote Myself

Four men
And two women
Will be seated at the table.
The man who invited you
Will soon
Tell you—
He is interested in another.
You do not know
You are no longer safe
Under the impression of
Being his date.
You do not know
But you are now a target.
An open house
At which you do not know
You are on the market.
The man seated next to you
When he is asked
During his question of truth
Will admit you are the one
In the room
He would choose
To sleep with.
The one seated at the end
Will kiss you on his dare
Without hesitation.
He will later confess
He would love
To take you to bed
But you did not want
This information.

Your brain will not know
How to cope
With all of this
Unwelcome attention.
The worst of it all—
The man who will later
Assault you
You do not even remember
There being a conversation.

Men will criticize
The amount
Of make up around your eyes
To make you think
You need their validation.
They will bring out drinks
You will not think
To watch being poured
Until after they are already
In your stomach.
They will not be
The only thing
That makes you feel sick.
Please know
None of this means
You were asking for it.

A Song I Wrote in the Shower

They say the best
Is yet to come.
Well maybe that's true
But when is it due?
Because I've been waiting
For so long.

I've been to Hell and back.
It burnt up my soul and
My shoes.
They didn't even come off—
He didn't need them to.

I looked for Heaven
In a set of eyes
Ocean blue
But he left me for dead
And I couldn't see an afterlife
Even if I wanted to.

I finally found
A show I can watch
That does not make me want
To turn the T.V remote
Into a ring toss.
That does not make me bitter
Resenting the displays of happiness
Of which—
I feel I was robbed.

Perhaps it helps that it is about
A young, female assassin
With a knack for chopping off
What all women contemplate
When their husbands have been
Staying at the office too late.

A part of me wishes
She wasn't a character
But someone real
Because I know a guy
For who I think she could
Cut a good deal.

Returning to my college town
But this was not a homecoming.
It is as though
I keep stepping back
Further in time.
Revisiting old stomping grounds
I thought I had left long behind.
But my friend's couch
Was the safest place
I have felt in a while.
Words of support are
So much stronger
When the phone does not have to be dialed.

They warned me
About returning memories
But I did not expect them
To be quite as unsettling.
To make it seem
This had been
Far darker than I thought
Originally.

Could it be they tricked me
Into that room
Under the guise of a game?
Was the man who invited me
An oblivious narcissist
Or do the two of them
Love to collaborate?
Was this—
A practiced play?

Looking back
There are so many things
I did not think twice of
But now intrude my dreams.
I thought that he
Was simply being kind
When he insisted
He retreat to the kitchen
To fetch me red wine
Even though I said
I was fine
Drinking the bottle of white
Already open
On the table in sight.

He said it was no problem
But then why did he need
His friend to go with him?
If it was that easy
Why did he snap his hands
To get his attention?
If he knew this apartment
Thick-and-through
What were they doing
Or saying
Before he brought my drink out
To the living room?

-Red flags are never black-and-white.

He is asked for
His truth
The question—
How many women
Has he slept with?
More than fifty.
Less than one million.
We all laughed
But looking back
I wonder if this is
Simply a number of women
Or of crimes he has committed?

-Is there even a difference?

He is the only man I know
Who can say he is guilty
Of breaking-and-entering
In his own home.
He is the only man to whom
I've been introduced
Who is guilty of robbing someone
Inside his guest bedroom.

The Difference Between Sleaze and Deceit

He said he did not have
Great English
Before our first date.
Tell me why his other cousin
Questioned why we were speaking Spanish
If I was *'from the States?'*
Tell me why I found his blog
From years ago
Where he writes perfectly
As if—
For a magazine?
Tell me why he lied
About his mile-wide vocabulary?
Tell me why
Everyone spoke English
At the event he described
As a cultural gathering?
Why he chose to switch back to Spanish
The times he took shots at my self-esteem?
Or when I was trying to understand
What his intentions had been from the beginning?
Tell me why he now plants broken English
In his scripted Facebook pleas
As though I am too stupid to see.

-The fog has been lifted, but he is still in the dark.

He tangled me in his web
To have me come undone.
He is the criminal
Yet I am on the run.

I remember now
The white light
At the end.
I do not know if
Someone left
Or if he had entered again.
But the sliver of light
From the door ajar
Was the closest thing
To heaven.
Illuminating him enough
To stop and see.
Returning to my body at once
I was able to hit him away
And leave.

Though this was my worst nightmare
I am grateful someone woke me up.

-Guardian angels.

He may have been skilled
At covering his tracks
But that all would change
When I walked across
The welcome mat.
He is in
For an unwelcome surprise.
Though older
He is not wise.
He will have both his hands
And his tongue tied
Trying to find an exit door
To the crime scene
Of his own making.

-There is no white light to guide him.

When you use
People as pawns
You only play yourself.

I thought that I was testing him
When we first met
Back then.
I did not realize
I was the one being studied.

-Examining the truth.

Does his soul retreat
When the sun leaves?
Was he evil by design?
Or did the poison
One day simply
Arrive?

How could I not see
As a thief
He—
Could not express
Buyer's remorse?

I may have to live
With what he did
For the rest of my life
But he is his own prisoner:
Forever hostage to
His gluttonous appetite.

-I hope he starves.

He broke inside my frame
Though he is no work of art.
His painted picture hangs
In the hallway.
I should've known
He was criminally vain.
But there is one truth
I cannot tame.

I do not know
How many men
Came and went
For they all said something about me
Which was sexually explicit.
I fear I will never know
Who was complicit
In breaking me apart.

My mind only preserves parts
And they made sure the room was dark.

I have spent
A considerate
Amount of time
In my head
Wondering
How I can make sure
This never happens
To me again.
Am I too shy?
Too delicate?
I thought I was refined
But perhaps this
Sensitive heart
It only made me
The perfect target.

Though it was a setup
This was not a blind date.

Though I could not see
I was still bait.

She says she
Is not worried
About me.
My radar to sense
What is dangerous
Still works.
That this is
A matter of misfortune.
Of meeting evil
In a form in
Which you
Have not been warned.
On a field
Which is not level.
I now understand
What they mean
By the phrase
Handsome devil.

When I look back I think
Maybe it was a blessing
I could not scream
Because this was his home.
His guests mingled outside.
If it came down
To keeping me quiet
To preventing an unwelcome surprise
I am not sure
I would have made it out of that room
Alive.

After something
So extreme
How do I learn
To trust—
To believe
Any kind word
From a man
Is not part of a plan
Or sinister scheme
To bait
And later
Break me?

They say to forgive
But never to forget.
How I long to do
The opposite.
I search for a sponge
To scrub my mind clean
And a pint-sized boxer
To kick-back
All my memories.
I bought a pill-sized bouncer.
He tells the thoughts
To get lost
But he must not
Be very good at his job
Because they come back
Without fail each time
And they always find a manner
To cut the line.

I must retrain
My body and brain
To understand
They are no longer in danger.
They are still
On high alert
Unable to shut down
These protective nerves.
I can yawn during the day
But the tension returns
In dark rooms
When I try to lay
My head down to sleep.
Tell me how a defense lawyer
Can argue against biology?
Against the primitive
Fight-or-flight wired inside of me?

It is a wild thought
That they can ignore
What my body cannot.

I wake up
In yet another
Hot sweat
With a racing heart
Like I am panicked
To be alive—
To be awake.
My body still
Does not know it is safe.
They say
My brain is hard at work
Processing the trauma
When I am asleep at night.
Trying its hardest to make sense
Of a senseless crime.

The strange thing about bad people is
They often find each other.
The scary thing about bad people is
They often find you.

I go from sad to angry
Then to furious
To depressed.
I smile sometimes
Talking to baristas in line
Then run to the bathroom
To momentarily cry.
I go from 'I can conquer anything'
To 'I cannot even conquer sleep.'
I go from speaking to strangers
At book signings
To avoiding eye contact
On family outings.
I go back to black
To blue
To red
To punching walls
To restlessness.
My god, it is exhausting
Feeling
All of this.

I cringe when I think about
How you asked me if my roommates knew
I was on a date with you.
How I laughed
Telling you that—
It was only to make sure
You were not a psychopath.

I am still not sure to this day
If it is true
But whether or not you
Are a psychopath
It does not mean
They are not in
The company you keep.

Social Media Sociopaths

I realize now
And it scares me
Just how—
Many victims
Could be out there.
How many ot*hers*
Have they hurt?
On all the trips
They say are for work.
Business trips
Where they
Can be on a plane
The very next day
Never to be held
Accountable
To the women they owe.
How many women are there
Who—
Never even knew
Their last names?

They hide who
They really are.
Using initials
For the power to disappear
Near or far.
So they have the power to
Delete a woman
Off of a dating app.
Never to
Look back.

So they have the power to
Block her on Instagram
So she can never identify him.
So they have the power to
Block her number
So she has no way of
Reaching him after.

*-He said it was to protect his
privacy from employers, yet he
has been able to legally drink
for almost a decade.*

I wondered today
What is the least offensive way
To talk about
Rape?
What is the least aggressive way
To say
Sexual *assault?*
But then
I realized how ridiculous it is
To try not to step on toes
With my tongue.
I realized the absurdity
That lies
In trying to beautifully package
A hideous crime.

The embassy
Did not answer the phone
When it was an emergency.
But Washington called
My mother back
Before she could blink
One month later.
Already familiar
With my story
And my night in danger.

But they will only admit
Their mistake
That the only lifeline I had
Was not awake
That he had left
The phone on vibrate
In a soundproof room
In which phones cannot
Enter with you.

There is a new girl
Living in my room.
They say she is
An American too.
Does she know?
She is enjoying the fruits—
Of my labor.
Does she know?
About the bed bugs
I had to fight.
That she will never have to
Be woken up by bites
Or put everything she owns
Into trash bags
To be carried down
Three flights
Of stairs.
That she will not have
To bear
Nights in front of
Coin laundry machines.
She does not even know
She should thank me
Or that I would go through
Another infestation
If it meant
I got to hug
My roommates again.

If it meant
I could laugh with my friends
One last time.
She does not know those bugs
Were not the worst monsters
Under this bed of mine.

Devil's Advocate

I thought the girl at the end
Was sent
To rescue me.
To help me gather my things
At a time when
My mind
Was not functioning.
At a time when
My body
Was still frozen.
Unable to comprehend—
How to escape
The situation
I was in.

But now I fear
That all along
She was simply
Another pawn.
Making sure that I would leave
After he instructed me.
Following that kitchen scene
It was clear I was
Too much of
A liability.

She asked if I
Wanted to talk about things
But was this to see
If I was okay?

Or what I would
Be able to say
I remember?

She forced me to put
My number in her phone
Only for me to later reach out
And her to say, *it's best*
If I leave things alone.
Waiting an entire day
To plan out what to say
Only to suggest—
I speak to my rapist.
That that is what
She would do
If she were in my shoes.
She does not know
Those shoes
Sit inside a bag
In my lawyers'
Office room.

And I wonder what it is
That caused her
To flip a switch
Or was it always
Like this?
Was she just another
Reinforcement?

156

I don't want to think
About this anymore.
My mind will not give up
Trying to find a conclusion.
Trying to find logic
In something that does not
Make sense
Because there is no reason
To explain this.
I cannot understand
The brains of
People who are sick
When my heart has always been healthy.

What happened to me
Is unbelievable.
Maybe that is
What makes it so easy—
For no one to want to
Believe me.
What happened to me
Is unbelievable.
Believe me
I have tried
Relentlessly.
I have lost my mind
Trying—
To process
To make sense of it.
To find logic
In a horror
I cannot comprehend.
What happened to me
Is unbelievable.
I could not try
To dream it up.
It is a nightmare
From which I cannot wake up.

Oh god it hurts.
I am so deft
At using words
But that night
I could not speak
Beyond
Wait
What
What are you doing?

-The grudge I hold against my own tongue.

Wait
What
What are you doing?
He asks as he
Is finally—
Called to testify
Before the judge.
Funny how
I imagine those words sound
Now
When they come
From his mouth
Not mine.

Thank you to
The lawyers who
Are committed to
Justice.
Not just
Another paycheck.

-For you I am eternally grateful.

I attend trauma yoga
And the other survivor mentions
Her new job
And boyfriend
And I cannot help
But feel envy
Rise—
Inside of me.
I feel guilt bubble
For I do not even know her story
Yet here I am
Filled with jealousy
For all of the things
That no longer feel possible for me.

I sit at the crisis center couch
And I try not to stare
At those who walk through the door.
But each time I see a new face
I understand that there is
More diversity among rape
Than on most office floors.
It does not limit itself
To gender
Age
Or race.
I realize even I
Don't understand
The reality of this epidemic
We are in.

-On how much we need to focus on spreading information.

The Only Thing 'We Ask for' Is to Be Heard

If you did not
Get the help you need.
If you did not
Go to the police
It does not mean
It did not happen.
(Know this, please)

If you were in a relationship
It does not mean
He was entitled to it.
If you were not in the mood
If you have had
Too much to consume
He should have never
Touched you.
*(Please do
Not question your rights to
Your own body)*

If you wore a short skirt
If you wore a tight shirt
It does not mean
He is free
To enslave your body.
Unwelcome sex
Should never be
Greeted by society
As something for women
To expect.

As though—
There are invisible boxes
We check
To qualify that she must have
Been asking for it.
In what way
Should another person
Be able to claim
We do not know
Our own wants
Better than they?

If you do not know
If you even slightly suspect
Leave her body alone
It is not
That difficult.

Do not tell me about urges
Men 'cannot control.'
If their brains are
Truly that simple
Why are they allowed
To serve in leadership roles?
When there are women
With the power to control
The urge to scream in ears
Who hear—
But do not believe her?

Denying another woman's story
Does not make you safe.
It only works to increase
The danger you face.
It only allows the problem to
Continue to perpetuate.
So please
If you care about the safety
Of your sisters and daughters
Believe what women say.
Protect one another.

Do you have some change to spare?
The world is broke
-And I am broken.

Slow down world.
You have not been making sense.
You are running out of change.
You have spent
Too much of your people
And not enough on them.

Stand-up comedians
I beg you to sit down.
To take the 'r' word
Out of your mouth.
I think it is time
You stop using
Gender-based violence
As a punchline.
You do not realize
Sexual assault
Is the least sexual crime.
It is not about
The men who 'just can't help themselves.'
It is about the women who can't.

-Cultural in-appropriation.

Society thinks
Women who look a certain way
Deserve rape
Yet use a man's appearance
To define
His capability of committing
This crime.
Society holds a woman responsible for
The crimes committed against her
When she is incapacitated
Yet excuses a man
For his violence
When he himself is
Under the influence.

-Phallic Fallacies.

Just because a man
Is not convicted
That does not mean
He is truly innocent.
What it does mean
Is that through all of
The pain and the shame
A court case brings
A brave woman persisted.

A drunk driver
Is shamed more for his *accidents*
Than a sexual predator's acts
Backed by *intent.*
Why do we
Consent,
To this?

I Am Not Sorry If This Makes You Uncomfortable

I was fine
Until he got
His hands on me.
It has been two months
And still I find it hard
To cope with the fact
He thought he could
Do what he wanted
With my body.
That I did not have a say.
That although a stranger, he
Was somehow
Entitled to me.

And if I slow my focus
What I try my hardest
Not to notice
Gets it to have
Its way with me too.
I'm forced to
Acknowledge
My own innocence.
This sad fragility
Of not knowing
The violence
In his positions.
The tactics
Of catching you off guard
Employing the dark
As a weapon.

Of being blindly dragged
By the hips.
My face pressed against walls:
A real-life *Blair Witch Project.*

His grotesque grunting
When you cannot defend
Yourself against him.
When you are not an active
Moving participant.
Wondering after
This cannot be
Simply
How two people
Show love.
(Can it really?)

To wonder if it is uncommon
To go up to
The man who
You lost your virginity to
Trying to understand
What just happened to you.
How you ended up
In that room?
Because even then
Perhaps twenty—
Maybe only ten
Minutes after
You still cannot remember.

When the woman you told
Seeking help
Decides to scold
You
Making you wonder
If this is just
A new way
People make—
Love?

I had no reference
No comparison
To know what had happened
Had not been
An act of drunken sex.
That I had not been
In some way asking for it
But that this
Was violence.

I had no reference then
To know that
Two people don't
Intertwine bodies when
One is not
Of conscious mind.
When she can't see
Where he is
And has slow reaction times.
To know that one person
Does not take
The phrase
What are you doing?
As a green light
To ignore her

And force his way inside.
To know that two people don't
Meet bodies
In the absence of kisses.
Without previous
Conversation
Even if only spoken in
Body language.
Usually you would think
You would have enough time
To speak
Or the ability to physically see
His intentions
Before he silences you
With the shock-inducing pain
Of an unwelcome entrance.
In a tango-for-two
Usually your clothes
Are removed.
Usually sheets are involved.
Usually your head lays upon
A pillow.
Usually you are not an animal
Playing dead.
Usually you
Are not dragged to
The foot of the bed
To be shaken and spread
By aggressive hands.
Hands he will use on
Monday morning's
Office meetings.

*-And these are only the things I
can remember.*

My feelings fluctuate
More than the numbers
On the scale.
And it is so surreal
To feel—
As though maybe
I can continue
My original dreams
Interrupted—
By his schemes.
That maybe
In returning
I can reclaim my power
And the city.
That maybe
I can learn to command
Not to fear those streets.

I think about how
In nine months
A woman can bring
Life into this earth.
Maybe in nine months' time
I too can experience
A rebirth.
A second chance
At the life I deserve.

I volunteer
To teach English
To immigrants and refugees.
My co-teacher
Reaches out to me.
He wants to meet
For lunch or coffee
And though my schedule
Is wide open
I do not feel free enough
To meet a stranger
In a public place.
And I wonder if this fear
Will subside
Or if this feeling will follow me
For the rest of my life?

I am so scared
Of my first day
Facing strangers.
These new students
What will I say?
This is the first time
I am afraid
Of having to give an introduction.
Fearing the phrase—
Tell me about yourself.
A question I used
To light up a room
Or a first date
With my answer.
But now I don't know
Who I am or what I stand for.
The room is dark inside
And so am I.

I can no longer
Remember
The physical sensation
Of the pain.
I think it is incredible
What your brain
Can do
To protect you
During attacks on your body.
It is the same way
My uncle cannot remember
How it felt
To be enveloped in flames
After his boat exploded
With him on board its frame.
Or why the man on TV
Said he could not feel
The bear's teeth
As it was scalping him.
Or the woman
Who had not known
She had been stabbed
Eleven times
Due to the adrenaline.

Though different
We are all connected by
What has been long defined
By evolution.

Swan Song

I hope this ages you
The way it has me.
I hope it makes your hairline
Waltz backwards
And further recede.
I hope it stamps crow's feet
Around your empty eyes.
I hope your neck hurts
From tensing itself at night.
I hope that you do not sleep
While waiting
For your day in court
And even after
If they close the case
I hope that you will have aged
Enough that you
Will have to
Retire your wicked ways.

I am not afraid of the court questioning me
Regarding that night in December.
I am afraid of the court's questioning
Of my character.

Time Out

My lawyers have to coach me
Before my day in court
But I have never been
Very good at sports.
These are not the type
Of practice questions
I have ever had to answer in school.

I wonder why
I feel afraid.
Why I feel as though *I*
Have to watch what I say.
And I realize my fear
Is rooted in shame.

Though the ball is in my court
I worry about
Keeping my head in the game.
Though I do not have
To worry about
Keeping my story straight
I worry about
All of the ways
They will try to bend the truth.

If he does not respect my body's boundaries
What makes me think he will respect the rules?

I thought I had a way with words
That is until I met you.
Though I can paint a picture
With my mouth
Yours can bend the truth.

The consular officer
Says I am brave.
That she could not return to testify
If she were in my place
But she does not know
I do not always sound
As strong as I did today on the phone.
She does not know
About all of these poems
Or that I spent last night
In tears by the bath tub alone.
That this is not that simple.
That at the end of the day
I am still—
A girl in shoes I never wanted to fill.

How is it possible?

I ask the sky.

To feel so incredibly old

And like a child

At the same time?

How is it possible?

I ask the clouds.

To feel a current of fearlessness

And at the same time

A river of doubt?

My country now wants
To help me.
I think it is great
Until I reflect
On the man in the Oval Office
And the great lengths
He too went through
To keep a woman silent.
Until I reflect on the man
Society elects
To a seat
I view more sacred
Than that of a priest.
I realize how can I be so unfair
In my shaming of a country
When I am not even safe in my own?
When it is 2019—
And society
Makes the conscious decision
To look the other way
On these crimes?
Showing me
And others who have suffered
That we do not matter in their eyes.

Due Healing Process

Will they pay more attention
To the words which come from my lips
Or the clothing I have worn to this?
Will they judge me on the things I state
Or the amount of makeup on my face?
Will they doubt me more
If I let my emotions escape
Or if I put on a brave face?
Why do I even consider these things?
Why do I still worry
That this is still someway
My fault?
I thought I was learning how
To move on
But now I believe my counselor
When she points to the trauma diagram
And says I am still in Stage One.

I arrived to the apartment
At six pm.
I would not get home again
Until ten—
The next morning.
I would go between
Three hospitals
And three police stations
Trying
To find someone
Who could help me.

My roommate had to
Be my voice
During the hours in which
Spanish
Sounded like white noise.
Yelling at the front desk
To nurses
Who turned their cheeks
Saying I could not be seen
Until I went to the police
As two police officers
Stood in uniform
Staring right at me.

She was my guide
When my mind was useless.
By the time we arrived
To the right location
After being directed to
A closed train station
Not two, but three
Hours had passed.

I had no choice
But to go back.
To spill—
Whatever fragments I had
In my memory
At that moment in time.
5:30 am—
The detectives
As tired as I
But this was mandatory
For a doctor to treat me.

Still in shock
I could not read
My own police report
Before signing
In a language
I could converse in
Hours before he touched me.

Five hours
One hospital visit later
I still could not sleep.
I had to wash him
Off of me.
I had to put my clothes
And my shoes in a bag
Cause I knew I could never
Look back at them.

-*When they ask why my police
report is inconsistent.*

I wonder how it will feel
Stepping off of that plane.
Will I run into a wall of fear?
Or feel as though
I have come to reclaim
These streets?
Will the air welcome me
With the smoke of cigarettes?
Or will it simply—
Steal my breath?
Will I be greeted
By happiness?
That I can
Do this?
That I could come back
In the fall.
I am so afraid
My legs will again shake
And I will not feel able to return at all.

That I will feel like a tree unrooted
That begins to wither.
That I will learn my mind is not strong enough
To combat all of these triggers.

How many times
To how many ears
Must I scream
To be taken seriously?
To get someone to care
That this happened to me?
I do not know
If I can take
Another door willingly
Slammed in my face.
How many men and women
Can consciously overlook
The violence and blood
That shook
My entire body and life
To its core?
Did I ever matter?
Or do I just not matter
Anymore?

I feel like a harp
Intended for angels' hands.
Yes
I was played
But only by the devil.
He has plucked
All of—
My heart's strings.
It no longer beats
Willingly.
It no longer sings.
There is no music
Inside of me
Unless you count
This funeral hymn.
My heart and I
We march
To a defeated rhythm.

I go to group therapy.
This week's theme: *self-compassion.*
The counselor speaks—
What makes you worthy?
A girl replies—
Nothing.
That she will never be
Skinny enough
Or pretty enough
To matter.
And I wish to tell her
That none of those things
Are the answer.
That external validation
Is a zero-sum game.
That you can feel happy, okay—
Even confident.
It only takes one person
To make you question
Whether anything you thought
Made you 'worthy'
Had ever really existed.

-I thought if I had been enough for him,
then surely he would not have allowed him to rape me.

It was as though
They were crafting their alibis
Before I would question why
They needed them.
The Chamuyero said
That he—
Would love to sleep with me
But he respected me too much.
(How considerate)

The man I thought I knew
Who had kissed me
In the living room
Barely two—
Months before
Made sure I knew
After a drink or four
He was not into me anymore.
(Perhaps he was later)

It was as though
They were doing
Damage control
So that when I would wake
In that dark room
Trying to piece together
Who—
Could have had
Such malicious intent
I would have crossed them
Off the list.

They made sure my glass
Was always half-full.
Perhaps that is
The curse of
The optimist.

I look at myself in the mirror
And I ask her
Who do you think you are?
It must have been so easy for him
To see you as worthless when
No man, nor woman
Decided you had any value after.
When no one your heart screamed to
That your body had been broken into
Cared enough to see that your wounds
Were looked to.
When no justice system
Thought you deserved
A *just* chance
To be heard.
Sure
You do not know who you are now
But who did you think you ever were?

That night he broke my body
But not my heart.
Everyone else
Took care of that part.

He is the man in my dreams
Not of them.
It seems obscene
For me to call them
Dreams.
They more closely exhibit
One long, bad trip.
The offspring—
Of the traces of poison
He left in me.

For so long my only dream
Was to fall in love.
Now I am afraid
To fall asleep.
I am getting dangerously close
To being unable to discern
My nightmares from reality.
Unable to separate—
The sinking feeling at bay
When I am awake
From what I face
When it is pressed to
The pillowcase.
They act as though
This was a minor falling out.
My god—
When will my hair
Stop falling out?

Even if the law
Makes things right
Will there be anything
Left of me?

I am so afraid
By the time the leaves
Return to the trees
I will still not have sight
Of a future.
That this body
Will not feel
Like a home.
I am afraid of a day
When my poems
Turn into a single note.

I collapse under the weight
Of crooked scales.
My back has become
Their bookmark
In a checkbook.
Perhaps this is the lost art?
Of letting a thief off the hook.
Letting him steal a piece
In the gallery
While they nail your hands to the frame.

How messed up is it
That I question
Whether I am being dramatic?
Whether I am asking for too much
In wanting the man
Who violated me
To have to be held
To a standard of accountability?
Why was it so easy for him
To force his way inside my body?
But so difficult for me
To try to seek
Justice?
How can this be
The way it *just is?*
I dare to ask is it easier
For a man to get away with murder?
Than it is
To live—
As the woman rises from the dead to report it?

I wish I believed in a God
Because then I would feel
He would have a real judgement day.
But part of me laughs
Because even then—
He would buy
Indulgences.

I do not have pretty metaphors
Or flowery adjectives
To describe the pain
In my eyes
That has been told
To take a seat.
I am at a loss for words
To describe the hurt
Inflicted *by him*
By her
By every police officer
By the doctor
By the judge.
I do not have
More truth to speak
Than that I do not have
Anything—
Left to give
Besides up.

People think this is something
From which you can just
Move on.
I ask them
To listen.
To see that they
Are greatly wrong.
I have been stabbed.
I have been greatly injured.
A knife in my side
Would have been preferred
To the pain of a stranger
Trespassing a temple
He was not destined to enter.
In which
No one had worshipped.
I have been robbed
Of my human right to security.
Of the ability to trust anyone
To let them close to me.
My freedom to live in a home
I had wanted
To call my own
Has been revoked.
That night I was stripped of everything
Besides my clothes
And I have never felt more naked.

Who am I to think
Men seated in court room chairs
Are drawn to the field to protect me?
They are blinded by the same
Urge as him.
Though he employs his in dark rooms
Though he works at odd hours
They both are controlled by the need to be
In positions of power.

I am so mad at a crime
That is able to steal
Every second of my time.
To occupy my mind—
Indefinitely
While the men who arranged
My reckoning
Do not for a second
Think of me.
They do not feel any remorse.
I am just another *par for the course.*
They are already in the process of
Grooming another victim
And I do not know what is worse—
Knowing I cannot save her
Or that I tried my hardest to first?

Each time I take two steps forward
They shove my face
To meet the earth
But this is not the first—
Time we have been introduced.
Each time I think I am beginning
To heal
The judicial system
Reminds me I am not a real—
Concern.
But I do not simply
Want to make progress.
I want
(expletive)
Due process.

My guard has always been
Up high
But that night
I could not juggle
Keeping out my eye
For the circus awaiting me inside—
That flat.
Inspecting three men
Looking for their red flags
When I did not know
I should have been
Worrying about *him.*

The reality is
I should not have
To spend any part
Of any night
Worrying about which man
May later try to force his way inside.
It would have been easier
To perform financial analysis.
Pardon my French
But what kind of (expletive) society,
Is this?

-Stranger Danger of the acquaintance.

Men assault women
Everyday
Because we have shown them
They can get away with it
Without ever facing
A consequence.

Our claims
Disappear faster than
Our senses of self-worth
As we watch men receive
Greater penalties
For not paying a bill on time
Or smoking
A cigarette inside.

So much goes
Unreported.
Even documented crimes
Grow stale over time
As though they were never recorded.
Backlogs of rape kits
Thousands—
Never to be tested.

It is the invisible plague
We pretend we do not face.
We need to wake up
Not tomorrow, *but today*.
Our society is sick.
Forget the flu shot.
This is the real epidemic.

The Only Substance You Have Is That Which You Abuse

I wish I could sit
Across the table
From you again.
There is too much anger
Seated in my eyes.
No business degree
Could help me manage it.

I imagine if
I concentrate
I could send
You up in flames.

There is enough rage
Within my fists
I believe I could
Expel vengeance from
These fingertips
But I am forced
To stick with
Piano keys
And banging soap dispensers
Onto bathroom sinks.
Though I long ~~to speak~~,
To scream—
In your face

I will have to stick
To highways.
Yelling my truth
To passing cars
Though I long
To pass this war
To you.

This anger should not
Be my burden.
I should not be
The one in
A perpetual state of hurting.

Tell me
How many others are there
Like me?

Maybe we—
Can help each other
Remove the weight we carry.

Maybe we—
Can use it
To finally bury you
The way you bury the truth.

I see on the police report
I was the hot gossip.
A conversation starter
To people I don't remember
Ever seeing their faces
Yet they remember
Traces
Of me.
I read about how
They were uncomfortable
With the news
She spread like wildfire.
That the abuse—
Made their shots
Just a little harder to swallow.
Did you know
That did not stop them though?
That rape kills you
But not the mood?
As they dance the night
And you away.
Relieved
You finally abandon the scene—
Alone.
They party for three more hours
Till the sun escorts them home.

You do not have to be an art critic
To get the impression
These are not good people.
The problem is—
Like a work made by an impressionist
You cannot see the big picture
Until you take three steps backwards.

My tally of thieves
Has moved up to two.
I afraid with new evidence
The veil will reveal—
It to be tallied
At three
But the reality is
They all had a part in breaking me.
They knew I was in that room.
They sat on couches
The whole time.
They talked about the blood
Leaking from my body
But not one person came
To find me
While I was being wrecked
For the third time.
I lost consciousness
As the minutes ticked by.
I left my scarf
In my panicked exit
And I wonder now
Who collected it?
But I left far more of myself
In that apartment.
I ran down those stairs
But it was not a Cinderella moment.

Devil's Advocate (Pt. 2)

I thought I had encountered
The devil in
Female form
But I was mistaken.
She is not a single person
But a twin.

I thought an angel had been
Sent to me
To help me
Gather my things
But she was only a means
Of convincing me to leave.
She was so shocked
To learn of the words
I said.
She comforted him.
She went out of her way
Promising him
She would intervene
To make it seem
Like he did not hurt me.
She did not want him
To have to worry.
That though she noticed
I had been absent.
That I was in a room
Visited by two men
On and off again
These must have all been
Misunderstood
Acts of consent.
That surely, I did not mean

What I had said I meant.
She does not know
These police reports
Are the first time I have
Had to learn
There was more than one man.
The first time I learn
My 'period' had been
A topic of sport
Thrown around
The living room
As the man she defends
Assaults me
For his round two.
That she was shocked
I did not reappear
But when later
I left the room, alone
I was assuredly
Mentally clear.
I was *'completely normal'*
As she found me alone
Supporting my head
On the kitchen counter
Missing my phone.

But I could not
Have been clear.
I must have misunderstood
Before—
When I said this man
Had turned my body
Into a war.

209

She told me to rest.
That tomorrow is
A brand-new day.
She helped me find my jacket
But it was he
She would cover up
Blanketing his mess of a bed
In which he now
Decides he does not want
To lay.

I text her thank you
For her help
As I lie in a hospital bed
While she lies in
Her police report
And leaves me on read.

Leonard

This was no Chelsea Hotel.
Yes, I got a way
But I was no one's babe.
It was only after
Hitting him away
That I could leave
But there was no limousine
Waiting out on the street.
An ambulance
Would have been
Just fine for me
Or maybe just
A shoulder on which to lean.

-I don't even have the music.

Saving Grace (Face)

I wonder how it is possible
To go from the Madonna
To the whore
In just a matter of hours?
Of choosing every dare
Out of being too timid—
Too scared
To confess—
Sexual inexperience
Only to have
To have a stranger later
Do everything but undress—-
You
Not once, but twice
As you must admit
You can barely remember
The first
Time he did
Or was that the second?

As you fall to your knees
Praying that they are lying.
That *they* or *he*
Could not have done
This more than once.
Giving himself
An intermission
As he lets another man
Cut in
In front of so many eyes
As you never reappear.
To hear that so many ears
Heard your claims

That he hurt me
That I'm bleeding
That I am not okay
Only to apologize
To their guests
For you making them
Uncomfortable
With the things you say.

For feeling guilty
That they invited you
Because look dear,
He has ruined your body—
But you have ruined the party.

For sending girls
You thought were
Your saving grace
But we're really there
To save face.

For assuring you leave
While he goes
To buy a pack of smokes
On the corner of the street
As though everything
That occurred
Had just been part of
A normal routine.

To confess
They noticed
You had been missing

Saying you disappeared
Into a bedroom
Visited by not one man
But two
And they just thought
Sure it seemed like something
You must always do.

Even though you plead
After
Wondering how
Your body can go
From gold
To sold in one—or was it two
Or three encounters?

You thought your first time
Would have its quirks
But nonetheless
It would be priceless.
You did not know
But now you and your body
Are both—
Worthless.

You thought when it happened
It would be unforgettable.
Funny perhaps.
Yes
It will haunt you forever

But there are no laughs.

Witness Stand-Up Comedy

The police officers write
This does not look like
A criminal offense
After only speaking
With two people
On his personal defense.
Coordinating—
Collaborating—
Reports so transparent
They make my pale skin
Seem opaque
Even though
The naked eye bathes
In rivers of blue veins.

They do not see suspicion
In the man who was written
By them
Into my bedroom.
A man who—
Does not even enter the scene
In what I have stored
In my memory
Or my original reporting.
A man who refuses to answer
When the police
Knock at his door
In the form
Of phone calls
And written letters.

He may have entered my body
Too—
But he has left the country.
I don't even know
If he will return.
I don't even know
If I will
Get the turn
To look the judge in the eyes
And speak my truth.
Though the only man
I know for certain
Clarified
By his own admission
Violated me
Not once
But twice
In one night
Gets to add more lies
To his side.
Standing at his hearing
With his head held high
As he attains a
Personal high
From painting
A false image
Of himself as a martyr
And one of myself
As a hysterical woman

*-But I don't find this funny
at all.*

Their reports only poke
More holes—
In their story
But the police officers
Do not like to spend their time
Digging.

*-They would rather bury you in
paperwork instead.*

I meet a charming boy
On Valentine's Day.
Three months ago
It would have seemed
Like a dream
But in the present
I cannot stop fear from rising.
My head instantly
Floods with the thought
What is he hiding?
What does he want
From me?
He offers to buy me a drink
And I have to bite my tongue
To keep from interjecting
Only if I see it being poured!
My heart can no longer
Trust hands will hold it anymore.
He asks me what I do
And my mouth still has not
Mustered up an excuse.
My life is still undefined
And who am I
Without a definition?
Each act of kindness
Is accompanied by suspicion.
How do I know
He won't turn out
To be like *him?*
My blood and I can never
Be positive.

-Does he want to sweep me off of my feet,
Or onto my back?

What happened to me
Slips out of my mouth
Before I can stop it.
Emotional word vomit
I want to endlessly apologize for
Until I realize all the women
I feel sorry for telling
Often say they too—
Have had an assault happen before.
And I wonder just how many of my friends
And my acquaintances
Have suffered for so long
In silence?
I have begun to run out of hands
Still we seemingly can
Always count on violence.
These numbers do not make me want
To speak up.
They make me want to stand up
And scream—
Enough is (expletive) enough.

I guess this loneliness in my heart
Does not yet mean
I am ready for dating.
News of my assault
Still slips off of my tongue
And onto my plate
During—
Tipsy guesses
Drunken confessions
On the first date.
And though he says
He does not scare easily.
Though he wants to line up
Date two
Before the end of the evening
I should not be surprised
That he dropped off
Once he sobered up
And saw I had too much baggage
On my plate.
And I feel it to be my fault
He is not hungry enough
To bare the taste.

-He paid for everything, but I am the one paying.

My students are a class of women
Striving to better their lives
And the lives of their children.
I show them it is okay
To make mistakes
By proving I too
Am afraid
Of speaking a foreign language.
By the end of the class
We have all shared two hours
Filled with comfortable laughs
And though my hands shook
When I wrote
The woman's name
Similar to *his* on the board
I could not help but feel
Though these women
Are improving their lives—
Their presence is my reward.

I attend a fashion panel alone.
They speak of a famous designer.
One I barely know
But this was just a way
To force myself to leave
The house this week.
And I can't help but feel
A flutter in my heart
And water form
A birdbath in my eyes
As they speak
About his work being
Polarizing.
That in being true
And taking a risk
Some people will hate
The fact you exist
But the ones who love you
Will love you with a love
So intense
It will make all your sacrifices
Worth it.

-This makes me feel brave enough to share my story.

I was a flower child
  In a garden of weeds.

Searching for sacred soil
  In a world of thieves.

I spend each day
Writing in coffee shops
But I will no longer
Be written off.
I will no longer be defined
By anyone else's words.
I will live my life
On my own terms.

I live my life like an open book.
Perhaps it is because I refuse to be
Anyone's coffee table coaster.

<u>Things I can now do:</u>

1. Mail letters and post cards to my friends overseas.
2. Skype A for therapy.
3. Go to trauma counseling twice a week with J.
4. Teach English to immigrants and refugees in the community.
5. Practice Spanish with them to show them I am a student too.
6. Go to trauma-informed yoga on Wednesdays.
7. Make other survivors laugh at group therapy.
8. Meet strangers at book signings.
9. Get invited to participate in art shows by those strangers.
10. Meet Z in Paris for the Spring break I always dreamed of.
11. Feel safe in coffee shops surrounded by people.
12. Chat with the baristas about shark attacks.
13. Try out modeling to feel comfortable again in my body.
14. Join a creative community of strong women.
15. Sing in front of strangers on Tuesday nights.
16. Write this book.
17. Heal.
18. Try to make beauty from the blood.
19. *Not take shit from anyone ever again.*

What good is a voice
That is not used for good?
What is the point in a voice
That does not point to
The truth?

Do not tell me I have pretty hair
Or compare—
The curl of my lips
To the handle
Of your favorite coffee mug.
I am not that easy to grasp.

Tell me about
The shards of glittering hope
Seated in my eyes
When I talk about the future.
Tell me about all the ways
They make you brave
Enough to lace
Your tattered shoes
And chase your own.

I am a survivor
Not a victim.
It is evident in
The scars on my knuckles
From falling outside
The third hospital
To turn away my roommate and I.
It is evident in
The bags
Under my eyes
Heavy with
Unkept promises
Between the universe and I.
I am wounded
But I am not broken.
I am quiet
But on this page
I am outspoken
For the sake of all the women
Who hide their pain.
For all the women
Who live with secret shame.
If you understand
This firsthand.
If you are seated
Take a stand
For you too
Have goddamned survived.

I am more than enough
But I am not too much.
I am fragile
But I am not shallow.
I am self-reflective
But I am not vain.
But most importantly—
I am who I am
Not who anyone says
I became.

You may cross boundaries
But I cross oceans
And it has come time
To drown your memory at sea.
Waves will break
And I will break free.

History

I have been made aware
Good people still comprise
A fair share
Of this earth
But the bad is magnified
Because crooked people
Do not fall by the wayside.
They continue to knock you
Onto your side
And claim that you fell.

They ask why I insist
In putting up such
A strong fight.
Should I not be satisfied
With knowing I survived?
But they do not see
I was not the first
Opportunity
He has snatched.
That I will not
Be his last.
That—
Bad people do not get a taste
Of the cold
And later decide
To hang up their coats.

They are comforted by
Their need
To commit crimes.
They will keep themselves
Covered
In plain sight
Until we decide
To open our eyes
To the future victims
Set to collect dust
On our mental shelves.
Until we decide to realize
Like history—
Mischief
Repeats itself.

I will keep moving
Even if it means
Treading water.
Even if it means
Swimming against their current.
Even if it means
Leaping between buildings
Or climbing uphill
In shoes whose soles
Have long worn thin.
I will keep moving
Even if I cannot sprint forward.
Even if I feel
As though I am falling backwards.
They will never gain
The satisfaction of keeping me still.
I will keep moving.
I will.
I will.
I will.

My luck has run out on me
But the hope in my heart
Will not budge its feet.
Firmly planted
I only can
Wait and see
If it will
Grow.

(Please.)

A love letter to my readers,

If you have made it to the end, I would like to say thank you.
My hope in sharing my story, is to keep the conversation going.
To keep society's ears open, so that together we can work to support
women and men who have been victims of an unimaginable crime.
To end the myths perpetuated by media, miseducation, and our natural
tendency to deny. To stop a culture present in countries who appear to
be westernized. Societies that resort to victim-blaming, failing to
provide them the support they need. Modern cultures which still refuse
to believe women due to the simple truth—*that we don't want to.*
Because believing women means,
Accepting the existence of evil in this world.
Because believing women means,
Accepting that we are not in control.
Because believing women means,
Accepting that if this can happen to me,
It can happen to you too.
That nobody is immune.

So please,
Join me.
Let's keep the conversation going.
Share this book with a friend.
Talk about it.
Don't be afraid.
This is how we fight shame.

XOXO Belle

You can follow Belle and the rest of her journey at
www.themorningregainingherglory.com

Find her on Instagram: @Bellejarpoetry

Made in the USA
Middletown, DE
20 May 2019